CONVECTION OVEN COOKBOOK FOR NEWBIES

Delicious, Finger-Licking and Budget-Friendly
Recipes for Your Countertop Convection Oven

Billie Mount

Table of Content

INTRODUCTION

Have you heard of an oven? This heating mechanism is a great
alternative to the traditional heaters, especially for your kitchen.
Convection ovens are smaller compared to the conventional ones. This
is because their air movement technology has lessened the need for
large ceiling areas. Unlike the conventional ones, these are specially
designed with a fan that circulates the air inside it. This mode of
heating is the most efficient one that has been developed to date. This
can be considered a much better option than the conventional ovens.
You must have heard the term 'low calorie', however, ovens do not
have low-calorie features but they do manage to consume less amount
of power.

Convection ovens cook almost six times faster than the normal stoves,
and not only does it reduce the cooking time, it also enhances the
flavors of the food. These ovens though small, are technically
advanced. The technology used in ovens is the same one that is used
on commercial airplanes to heat them. The convection heating system's
efficiency is highly dependent on the recipes used by the user. Of
course, the user has complete control over the level of heating and the
features of the oven. The specialty of an oven is that it starts cooking
the food from the top and the bottom surfaces and not just the top.
This gives not only the extra flavors but also prevents the disasters like
the burning of food as it keeps the food evenly warmed. This is
another great advantage of an oven. However, it is important to
correctly follow the instructions given when purchasing these ovens.
Convection ovens are great for people who wish to cook in bulk. This
depends on the user's characteristics. Small households may cook on a
regular basis, but someone who is fond of baking cookies or enjoying
baking bread will require an oven. This type of oven is also suited for

people who wish to use it for heating green stuff, for instance, for the use of a steamer. Another great advantage of this oven is that it can be used for cooking a whole meal. If the oven is of good quality, the dish can be cooked perfectly well and does not have the starchy taste or the burnt taste that is common with traditionally cooked food. The cooking process on this oven is much faster than other ceramic or traditional stoves. You should also note that this is significantly more energy efficient as it does not require more energy consumption than other types of stoves.

The oven is best suited for those people who feel that they would like to cook in huge batches of food. The choice of an oven depends on the intended use of the oven. You should choose the right oven for a particular purpose. Another advantage of the oven is that it makes the food come out perfectly by nourishing the food with liquid. This in no way requires you to thaw the frozen food in the traditional oven if you have frozen food for your oven. Of course, you should not cook frozen food on a normal heating device as it may turn hazardous.

In order to have the best out of your oven, you should follow the instructions to a T for safety measures. Before you purchase the convection oven, ensure that it is of a good quality. Ensure that the oven heats evenly. Also, ensure that it operates without making too much noise. It should also be very convenient for storage of the food. It should also be easy to clean.

Different Types of Convection Oven

There are several types of Convection Ovens; the most common types are divided into two categories. The first type is differentiated by the placement of the fan and additional heating element; this is the regular and the true convection oven.

The second type is classified by its placement or position in the kitchen; the major types are the countertop convection ovens and the floor models.

Regular convection oven

A regular convection oven is a device used to heat various types of food and beverages. A convection oven possesses several 'products' for delivering heat to the food placed in the oven.

True convection oven

A true convection oven is a natural method of cooking that is used in most restaurants. The cost of running a true convection oven is virtually nothing because they cut out the expensive internal electric or gas-powered convection fan, called a blower, which costs over $400 to replace. The idea behind the true convection oven is to use the air patterns that are naturally produced during cooking to distribute heat evenly to all areas of the oven.

Countertop convection oven

A countertop convection oven is like a countertop microwave. Instead of microwaves, it sends the hot air around and cooks the food from convection. And it has a door for the steam to get out.

Floor model convection oven

A floor model convection oven is a thing to envy. It's large enough to hold a 13"x9" cake tin, or the 8"x8" pan I use to bake brownies. The convection fan hubbub its blades mounted at the top of the dome-shaped door to mix the warm air as it cooks your meal.

It's a solid iron machine that makes my brownies with a crackling sound.

Breakfast

Baked Eggs

Preparation time: 5 minutes

Cooking time: 18 minutes

Servings: 6

INGREDIENTS:

- 6 slices of deli ham
- 1/4 teaspoon salt
- 1/4 teaspoon ground black pepper
- 6 eggs
- 3 tablespoons shredded cheddar cheese

DIRECTIONS:

1. Turn on the oven, set the temperature to 400 degrees F, and then select the oven cooking method.

2. Meanwhile, take 6 muffins cups, place a ham slice in it, and then crack an egg into each cup.

3. Sprinkle salt, black pepper, and cheese on top of each egg and then bake for 13 to 18 minutes until done.

4. Then switch on the broiler, continue cooking the eggs for 2 minutes, and then serve.

NUTRITION:

- Calories: 213
- Fat: 17g
- Carbs: 1g
- Protein: 14g
- Fiber: 0g

Sausage Patties

Preparation time: 5 minutes

Cooking time: 22 minutes

Servings: 8

INGREDIENTS:

- 1-pound breakfast sausage
- 1 teaspoon salt
- 1/2 teaspoon ground black pepper

DIRECTIONS:

1. Turn on the oven, set the temperature to 400 degrees F, and then select the oven cooking method.

2. Meanwhile, place sausage in a bowl, add salt and black pepper, and then stir until well combined.

3. Shape the mixture into patties, arrange patties on a parchment-lined baking pan and then bake for 10 minutes per side until cooked.

4. Then switch on the broiler, cook the patties for 2 minutes per side until browned, and serve.

NUTRITION:

- Calories: 182
- Fat: 15g
- Carbs: 1g
- Protein: 10g
- Fiber: 0g

Egg Stuffed Peppers

Preparation time: 5 minutes

Cooking time: 30 minutes

Servings: 4

INGREDIENTS:

- 4 medium bell peppers
- 1/4 cup chopped green onions
- 1 teaspoon salt
- 4 eggs
- 1 cup shredded cheddar cheese

DIRECTIONS:

1. Turn on the oven, set the temperature to 375 degrees F, and then select the oven cooking method.

2. Meanwhile, prepare the peppers and for this, cut off their tops and then remove the seeds.

3. Crack the eggs in a medium bowl, add salt and cheese and then whisk until combined.

4. Pour the egg mixture evenly into the prepared peppers, sprinkle green onions on top, and then arrange them on a baking pan.

5. Bake the peppers for 30 minutes until the top turn golden brown and when done, let them rest for 5 minutes.

6. Serve straight away.

NUTRITION:

- Calories: 151
- Fat: 5g
- Carbs: 8g
- Protein: 14g
- Fiber: 3g

Roasted Breakfast Potatoes

Preparation time: 5 minutes

Cooking time: 1 hour

Servings: 6

INGREDIENTS:

- 5 pounds red potatoes
- 1 medium green bell pepper, cored, chopped
- 1 medium white onion, peeled, chopped
- 1 medium red bell pepper, cored, chopped
- 3 teaspoons minced garlic
- 1 teaspoon salt
- 3/4 teaspoon smoked paprika
- 1/4 cup olive oil

DIRECTIONS:

1. Turn on the oven, set the temperature to 400 degrees F, and then select the oven cooking method.

2. Meanwhile, dice the potatoes into small pieces and place them in a large bowl.

3. Add onions, bell peppers, and garlic, sprinkle with salt and paprika, drizzle with oil and then toss until coated.

4. Spread the vegetables in an even layer on the baking pan and then bake for 1 hour until potatoes turn golden brown, stirring every 15 minutes.

5. Serve straight away.

NUTRITION:

- Calories: 275
- Fat: 7g
- Carbs: 49g
- Protein: 6g
- Fiber: 6g

Cinnamon French Toast

Preparation time: 5 minutes

Cooking time: 30 minutes

Servings: 6

INGREDIENTS:

- 6 slices of whole-wheat bread
- 1 teaspoon ground cinnamon
- 1 teaspoon vanilla extract, unsweetened
- 2 tablespoons butter, unsalted

- 3 eggs
- 1/2 cup maple syrup
- 1/2 cup milk

DIRECTIONS:

1. Turn on the oven, set the temperature to 350 degrees F, and then select the oven cooking method.

2. Meanwhile, take a 13-by-9-inch baking dish and then grease it with oil.

3. Arrange the bread slices in it in a single layer, and then sprinkle cinnamon on top.

4. Crack the eggs in a bowl, add vanilla, maple syrup, butter, and milk and then whisk until blended.

5. Pour the egg mixture evenly over the bread slices and then bake for 30 minutes.

6. Serve straight away.

NUTRITION:

- Calories: 218
- Fat: 8g
- Carbs: 32g
- Protein: 6g
- Fiber: 1g

Appetizers & Snacks

Beet Chips

Preparation time: 25 minutes

Cooking time: 60 minutes

Servings: 8

INGREDIENTS:

- 12 beets
- 2 teaspoons sea salt
- 1/2 cup olive oil

DIRECTIONS:

1. Turn on the oven, set the temperature to 300 degrees F, and then select the oven cooking method.

2. Meanwhile, scrub the beets, remove the top, and then cut beets into thin slices, about 1/16 inch thin.

3. Take a large bowl, place the beet slices in it, season with salt, drizzle with oil and then toss until coated.

4. Let the beet slices rest for 20 minutes, toss again, drain the liquid, and then spread the beet slices on the oven basket in a single layer.

5. Cook the beet slices for 60 minutes until crisp and golden, turning halfway and when done, cool the chips completely and then serve.

NUTRITION:

- Calories: 172
- Fat: 14g
- Carbs: 12g
- Protein: 2g
- Fiber: 3g

Kale Chips

Preparation time: 5 minutes

Cooking time: 25 minutes

Servings: 2

INGREDIENTS:

- 1/2 bunch kale leaves
- 1 teaspoon garlic powder
- 1/2 teaspoon onion powder
- 1/4 teaspoon of sea salt
- 1/2 teaspoon smoked paprika
- 3/4 teaspoon red chili powder
- 1 1/2 tablespoon nutritional yeast
- 1/2 tablespoon olive oil

DIRECTIONS:

1. Turn on the oven, set the temperature to 300 degrees F, and then select the oven cooking method.

2. Meanwhile, remove stems from the kale leaves, tore the leaves into large pieces, and then transfer them into a large bowl.

3. Drizzle oil over the kale leaves, massage each kale piece, add remaining ingredients and then toss until combined.

4. Spread the kale leaves on the oven basket in a single layer and then bake for 25 minutes until kale leaves begin to crisp.

5. When done, let the kale chips cool completely and then serve.

NUTRITION:

- Calories: 110.3
- Fat: 4.6g
- Carbs: 15.8g
- Protein: 5.3g
- Fiber: 5.6g

Zucchini Chips

Preparation time: 20 minutes

Cooking time: 6 minutes

Servings: 5

INGREDIENTS:

- 2 small zucchinis
- 1/4 teaspoon salt
- 1/4 teaspoon ground black pepper
- 1 cup panko breadcrumbs
- 1/4 cup grated parmesan cheese
- 1 egg

DIRECTIONS:

1. Turn on the oven, set the temperature to 350 degrees F, and then select the oven cooking method.

2. Meanwhile, remove the ends of each zucchini and then cut zucchini into round slices.

3. Spread zucchini slices in a single layer on a plate lined with paper towels and then sprinkle with salt.

4. Cover the zucchini slices with another layer of paper towel, place a heavy pot on top and then let it sit for 15 minutes.

5. Then place the breadcrumbs in a medium bowl, add salt, black pepper, and cheese and stir until mixed.

6. Crack eggs in a medium bowl and then whisk until beaten.

7. Working on one zucchini slice at a time, dip into the egg and dredge with breadcrumbs mixture until coated, and place on the baking pan.

8. Repeat with the remaining zucchini slices, spray oil on top and then bake for 6 minutes until golden brown.

9. Serve straight away.

NUTRITION:

- Calories: 95
- Fat: 3g
- Carbs: 11g
- Protein: 5g
- Fiber: 1g

Vegetables

Baked Macaroni and Cheese

Preparation time: 15 minutes

Cooking time: 30 minutes

Servings: 4

INGREDIENTS:

- 1/2 pound Cheddar cheese, shredded
- 4 tablespoon butter
- 2 eggs
- 1 teaspoon Dijon mustard
- 12 oz. evaporated milk
- 1-pound elbow macaroni
- Salt and black pepper to taste
- 1/2 cup breadcrumbs

DIRECTIONS:

1. Cook macaroni according to package directions.

2. Spray casserole dish with cooking spray.
3. Add all ingredients except for bread crumbs to a casserole dish and mix well to combine. Sprinkle with breadcrumbs.
4. Cover with foil and place pan on 1-inch rack. Bake on High (350 degrees F) for 15-20 minutes. Remove the foil, then cook for another 5-10 minutes or until golden brown.

NUTRITION:

- Calories: 480
- Total Fat: 19g
- Carbs: 31g
- Protein: 24g

Curried Zucchini Chips

Preparation time: 4 minutes

Cooking time: 22 minutes

Servings: 2

INGREDIENTS:

- 1 medium sliced zucchini
- 1 tablespoon virgin olive oil
- 1/8 tsp of garlic powder
- 1/4 tsp of curry powder
- 1/8 tsp of salt

DIRECTIONS:

1. Lightly grease paper-lined baking sheet. Arrange zucchini slices in one layer on the baking sheet. Sprinkle olive oil and dust with curry powder, salt, and garlic powder.

2. Place baking sheet on 1-inch rack and bake on High power (350 degrees F) for 12 minutes. Flip zucchini over and cook for another 10 minutes or till very crisp. Cool and store in an airtight container

NUTRITION:

- Calories: 152
- Carbs: 17g
- Fat: 3g
- Protein: 2g

Lemony Okra

Preparation time: 10 minutes

Cooking time: 20 minutes

Servings: 2

INGREDIENTS:

- 1 (10-ounce) bag frozen cut okra
- 1/4 cup nutritional yeast
- 2 tablespoons fresh lemon juice
- Salt and ground black pepper, as required

DIRECTIONS:

1. In a bowl, add the okra, nutritional yeast, lemon juice, salt, and black pepper and toss to coat well.
2. Arrange the okra into the greased oven basket in a single layer.
3. Turn on the oven and then adjust the temperature to 400 degrees F.

4. Set the timer for 20 minutes and press "Start/Stop" to begin cooking.
5. When the unit beeps to show that it is preheated, insert the basket in the oven.
6. When cooking time is complete, remove the okra.
7. Serve hot.

NUTRITION:

- Calories: 131
- Fat: 1.5g
- Sodium: 103mg
- Carbs: 20.1g
- Fiber: 9.6g
- Sugar: 2.4g
- Protein: 12.1g

Baked Sweet Potatoes

Preparation time: 10 minutes

Cooking time: 40 minutes

Servings: 2

INGREDIENTS:

- 2 large-size sweet potatoes
- 1 tablespoon of olive oil
- 1-2 teaspoons of sea salt

DIRECTIONS:

1. Wash the sweet potatoes, and using a metal fork, prick the potatoes to make holes.
2. Sprinkle olive oil over the potatoes and rub with salt.
3. Add the potatoes to the oven basket and bake at 390 degrees for 35-40 minutes, until fork-tender.

NUTRITION:

- Calories: 332
- Fat: 13g
- Protein: 25g
- Sugar: 12g

Seafood

Tuna Noodle Casserole

Preparation time: 20 minutes

Cooking time: 25 minutes

Servings: 4

INGREDIENTS:

- 5 oz. can tuna
- 10½ oz. creamy mushroom soup
- 1 cup egg noodles, cooked
- 1/4 cup cold water
- 1/2 cup frozen peas or green beans
- 2 tablespoon Breadcrumbs
- 1/4 cup sour cream
- 1/2 cup Cheddar cheese, shredded

DIRECTIONS:

1. In a large mixing bowl, combine together tuna, sour cream, green beans or peas, about 6 tablespoons cheese, cream of mushroom soup, and cooked noodles.
2. Mix well until it forms a cohesive mixture.
3. Pour the prepared mix into an 8-inch ovenproof dish.
4. Place the ovenproof dish on the 1-inch rack and cook on the 'HI' setting for about 18 to 22 minutes.
5. Once the timer is up, add the remaining cheese and breadcrumbs to the top of the semi-set casserole.
6. Bake on the 'HI' setting for another 2 to 3 minutes or until the cheese melts and gets light brown.
7. Once done, remove the casserole oven and allow cooling for about 7 - 10 minutes before serving.

NUTRITION:

- Calories: 367
- Total Fat: 11g
- Carbs: 25g
- Protein: 19g

Unusual Lime and Tequila Shrimp

Preparation time: 15 minutes

Cooking time: 25 minutes

Servings: 2

INGREDIENTS:

- 1 pound extra-large shrimp
- 3 tablespoon lime juice
- 2 tablespoon olive oil
- 2 garlic cloves, minced
- 2 tablespoon tequila
- 1/2 teaspoon ground cumin
- 1/2 teaspoon cayenne pepper
- Salt and ground black pepper to taste

DIRECTIONS:

1. In a large mixing bowl, whisk together lime juice, virgin olive oil, garlic, cumin, cayenne pepper, salt, tequila and pepper. Mix

well. Then add shrimps and marinate for 2-3 hours in the refrigerator.

2. Line bottom of NuWave Oven with foil. Place shrimp on the 4-inch rack. Cook on High Power (350 degrees F) for 3 minutes. Flip shrimp over and cook for another 3 minutes or until shrimp are opaque.

3. Serve and enjoy.

NUTRITION:

- Calories: 203
- Total Fat: 5g
- Total Carbs: 6g
- Protein: 19g

Tender Crab Cakes

Preparation time: 25 minutes

Cooking time: 35 minutes

Servings: 3

INGREDIENTS:

- 8 oz. lump crabmeat
- 2/3 cup panko breadcrumbs
- 1 tablespoon chopped parsley
- 2 tablespoon chopped green onions
- 1/2 teaspoon Old Bay seasoning
- 1/2 teaspoon Worcestershire sauce
- A pinch of salt
- 1/4 teaspoon cayenne pepper
- 1 teaspoon lemon juice

- 2 tablespoon mayonnaise
- 1 large egg
- 1 lemon
- 1 teaspoon Dijon mustard

DIRECTIONS:

1. In a large bowl, combine 1/3 cup breadcrumbs, parsley, green onions, Old Bay seasoning Worcestershire sauce, salt, cayenne pepper, lemon juice, mayonnaise, mustard, and egg. Add crabmeat and stir to combine well.
2. Place remaining breadcrumbs in a shallow dish. Form crab mixture into 3 equal size patties. Coat each side with breadcrumbs.
3. Place foil on 3-inch rack. Spray lightly with cooking spray. Place patties on foil. Bake on High Power (350 °C) for 6 minutes. Lip and cook extra 6 minutes.
4. Serve and enjoy!

NUTRITION:

- Calories: 260
- Total Fat: 18g
- Carbs: 13g
- Protein: 11g

Roasted Shrimp With a Herbed Salsa

Preparation time: 10 minutes

Cooking time: 18 minutes

Servings: 2

INGREDIENTS:

- 1 pound large shrimps
- 3 sliced garlic cloves
- 1 red Serrano pepper
- 1 bay leaf
- 1/2 lemon
- 3 tablespoon olive oil

For the Herb Salsa:

- 2 tablespoon chopped cilantro
- ½ tablespoon grated lemon zest

- 2 tablespoon chopped flat-leaf parsley
- ½ tablespoon virgin olive oil
- Kosher salt and black pepper to taste

DIRECTIONS:

1. Place the shrimp and Serrano pepper halves in an ovenproof dish, along with the bay leaf, garlic and virgin olive oil. Mix lightly till all the ingredients are well coated with virgin olive oil.
2. Place the baking dish on the 3-inch rack.
3. Cook on the 'HI' setting for about 3 to 5 minutes.
4. While the shrimp cooks, prepare the salsa.
5. Combine the cilantro, lemon zest and parsley together in a small mixing bowl. Season with salt and pepper to taste and stir to combine well.
6. Pour the olive oil over the salsa and let it stand for a few minutes before mixing it up.
7. When the shrimp is done, pour in the lemon juice and mix well to coat.
8. Serve the shrimp hot, topped with the prepared salsa.

NUTRITION:

- Calories: 163
- Fat: 3g
- Carbs: 2g
- Protein: 18g

Broiled Chipotle Tilapia

Preparation time: 10 minutes

Cooking time: 10 minutes

Servings: 2

INGREDIENTS:

- 1/2 lbs. tilapia fillets
- 1 teaspoon lime juice
- Cilantro, chopped
- 3 teaspoon chipotle
- 1 avocado, peeled and halved
- 3 tablespoon sour cream
- Mayo, 1 tablespoon

DIRECTIONS:

1. Blend the ingredients except for the fish.
2. Brush the fish fillets with the mix.
3. Broil the fish at 132°C or 270°F in your oven for 10 minutes.

NUTRITION:

- Calories: 385
- Carbs: 65g
- Protein: 18g
- Fat: 7g

Poultry

Turkey Breast

Preparation time: 5 minutes

Cooking time: 60 minutes

Servings: 6

INGREDIENTS:

- 4 pounds turkey breasts
- 2 teaspoons salt
- 1 tablespoon olive oil

For the Rub:

- 1/2 teaspoon paprika
- 1 teaspoon dried thyme
- 1/2 teaspoon dried oregano
- 2 tablespoons butter, unsalted

DIRECTIONS:

1. Turn on the oven, set the temperature to 350 degrees F, and then select the oven cooking method.

2. Meanwhile, prepare the turkey and for this, place all the ingredients for the rub in a small bowl and then stir until mixed.

3. Spread the rub gently under the skin of turkey breast, rub 1/2 tablespoon oil, season with salt and then rub remaining oil over the skin side.

4. Place chicken in the oven tray and then cook for 30 minutes per side until cooked.

5. When done, let the chicken rest for 10 minutes, cut it into pieces, and then serve.

NUTRITION:

- Calories: 361.2
- Fat: 11.1g
- Carbs: 0.2g
- Protein: 65.2g
- Fiber: 0g

Pork Chops

Preparation time: 10 minutes

Cooking time: 10 minutes

Servings: 4

INGREDIENTS:

- 4 pork chops, boneless, about 6-ounce, fat trimmed
- 1/3 cup all-purpose flour
- 4 cups cornflakes, crushed
- 1/2 teaspoon onion powder
- 1/2 teaspoon garlic powder
- 1/2 teaspoon paprika
- 1 teaspoon salt and more as needed
- 1 teaspoon mustard paste
- 1/3 teaspoon ground black pepper and more as needed
- 2 eggs

- 2 teaspoons water

DIRECTIONS:

1. Turn on the oven, set the temperature to 360 degrees F, and then select the oven cooking method.

2. Meanwhile, take a shallow dish and then place flour in it.

3. Crack the eggs in a separate dish, add mustard, 1/2 teaspoon salt, water, and then whisk until combined.

4. Take a separate dish, place crushed cornflakes in it, add onion powder, garlic powder, remaining salt, paprika, and ground black pepper, and then stir until mixed.

5. Season the pork chops with salt and black pepper until coated, dredge the chops in the flour, dip into eggs and then coat in the cornflake mixture.

6. Arrange the prepared pork chops on the oven basket and then cook for 10 minutes until thoroughly cooked, turning halfway.

7. Serve straight away.

NUTRITION:

- Calories: 400
- Fat: 22g
- Carbs: 22g
- Protein: 26g
- Fiber: 1.5g

Amazing Chicken Parmesan

Preparation time: 15 minutes

Cooking time: 30 minutes

Servings: 2

INGREDIENTS:

- 1 pound chicken breasts
- 1/2 cup seasoned Panko breadcrumbs
- 2 eggs
- 1/2 cup flour
- Salt and black pepper to taste
- 14oz. marinara sauce
- 1/2 cup Parmesan, grated

DIRECTIONS:

1. Beat eggs in a shallow bowl and lightly season with salt and pepper. Whisk well.

2. In another shallow bowl, put flour and season too.
3. In the third shallow plate, place the seasoned panko breadcrumbs.
4. Make light indentions on the chicken breasts with a sharp knife, making sure that you don't cut through.
5. Dip the chicken breasts into the seasoned flour. Then dip the flour-coated chicken into the eggs. Finally, dip the flour and egg coated chicken into the plate with the breadcrumbs and lightly press until the breadcrumbs stick to the chicken breasts.
6. Place the breadcrumb encrusted chicken on a 3-inch rack and back on the 'HI' setting for about 15 to 17 minutes per side.
7. Season each slice of chicken with Parmesan and continue baking on the 'HI' setting for another 2 to 3 minutes, or until the cheese melts.
8. Put the chicken breasts on serving plates, then slather the marinara sauce over them.

NUTRITION:

- Calories: 254
- Total Fat: 12.38g
- Total carbs: 12.18g
- Protein: 22.83g

Oven Fried Chicken Wings

Preparation time: 20 minutes

Cooking time: 25 minutes

Servings: 3

INGREDIENTS:

- 1 1/2 lbs. chicken wings
- 1/3 cup grated Parmesan cheese
- 1/3 cup breadcrumbs
- 1/8 teaspoon garlic powder
- 1/8 teaspoon onion powder
- 1/4 cup melted butter
- Salt and black pepper to taste
- Cooking spray

DIRECTIONS:

1. On a baking sheet, spray with cooking spray.
2. In a large bowl, mix Parmesan cheese, garlic powder, onion powder, black pepper, breadcrumbs and salt. Stir to combine well.
3. Dip chicken wings one at a time into melted butter and then into bread mixture until thoroughly covered. Arrange wings in a single layer on the baking sheet.
4. Place on 1-inch rack and cook on High power (350° F) for 10 minutes. Flip wings over and cook for another 10-12 minutes until no longer pink in the center and juices run clear. Remove promptly from NuWave Oven and serve.

NUTRITION:

- Calories: 371
- Total Fat: 22.6g
- Total carbs: 11.8g
- Protein: 27.8g

Bacon-Wrapped Chicken With Potatoes

Preparation time: 15 minutes

Cooking time: 28 minutes

Servings: 4

INGREDIENTS:

- 8 slices bacon
- 1 lb. baby red potatoes
- 4 bone-in chicken drumsticks
- 1 tablespoon dried basil
- 1/2 tablespoon garlic powder
- 1/2 tablespoon Italian seasoning
- 1/2 tablespoon black pepper
- 1 teaspoon salt

DIRECTIONS:

1. Wrap each piece of chicken with one slice of bacon.
2. Line bottom of NuWave Oven with foil.
3. Arrange chicken in the center of the 4-inch rack. Place potatoes around chicken on the rack.
4. In a medium-sized mixing bowl, combine garlic powder, black pepper, Italian seasoning, basil, and salt. Sprinkle seasoning mixture over chicken and potatoes.
5. Cook on High Power (350 degrees F) for 10 minutes. Turn chicken and potatoes and cook for another 10 minutes or until chicken is fully cooked and potatoes are tender.
6. Serve hot and enjoy.

NUTRITION:

- Calories: 542
- Total Fat: 14.8g
- Total carbs: 74.8g
- Protein: 32g

Garlic Ginger Chicken Wings

Preparation time: 20 minutes

Cooking time: 25 minutes

Servings: 4

INGREDIENTS:

- 2 pounds chicken wings
- 1 tablespoon vegetable oil
- A pinch of salt and black pepper
- 1 tablespoon Frank's Red Hot Sauce
- 1/3 cup flour

For glaze:

- 3 garlic cloves, minced
- 1 tablespoon Asian chili pepper sauce
- 1/4 cup rice wine vinegar
- 1 tablespoon minced ginger

- 1/4 cup light brown sugar
- 1 1/2 tablespoon soy sauce

DIRECTIONS:

1. In a large mixing bowl, combine Frank's Red Hot Sauce, vegetable oil, salt, and pepper. Add chicken wings and toss to coat thoroughly.
2. Place coated wings in a large zip lock bag. Add flour, seal bag, and shake until wings are coated with flour.
3. Place wings on the 4-inch rack and cook on High power (350 degrees F) for 10 minutes. Turn wings over and cook for an additional 8 minutes.
4. Meanwhile, in a large bowl, whisk together all ingredients for the glaze. Place wings in glaze and toss to coat evenly. Place wings back on the 4-inch rack and cook on High power for an additional 5 minutes.
5. Remove from oven, then serve.

NUTRITION:

- Calories: 312
- Fat: 7.5g
- Carbohydrates: 21.1g
- Protein: 18.8g

Chicken Thighs With Rosemary

Preparation time: 5 minutes

Cooking time: 35 minutes

Servings: 4

INGREDIENTS:

- 4 chicken thighs, with the bone and skin
- Rosemary sprigs
- A large potato, cut into cubes
- 1 onion
- 2 tablespoon of olive oil
- 2 garlic cloves
- Salt and pepper
- 1/2 teaspoon of chicken seasoning powder

DIRECTIONS:

1. Preheat the oven at 218°C or 425°F.
2. Put the rosemary sprigs on the baking pan with cooking spray.
3. Bake the remaining ingredients for half an hour.
4. Season the chicken thighs and bake for 35 minutes.

NUTRITION:

- Calories: 670
- Carbs: 14g
- Protein: 47g
- Fat: 46g

Baked Chicken Tenders

Preparation time: 25 minutes

Cooking time: 20 minutes

Servings: 6-8

INGREDIENTS:

- 1-1/2 lb. of boneless chicken tenders
- 2 eggs
- 2 teaspoon of butter, melted
- 2/3 cup of graham crackers
- 2/3 cup of breadcrumbs
- Salt and pepper for seasoning

DIRECTIONS:

1. Preheat the oven to 232°C or 450°F and spray some oil on the baking pan

2. Combine the crackers, breadcrumbs, and butter until smooth.
3. Beat the eggs in another bowl with salt and pepper.
4. Dip the chicken pieces in the eggs first and then the breadcrumbs.
5. Bake for 15-18 minutes.

NUTRITION:

- Calories: 362
- Carbs: 16.5g
- Protein: 58g
- Fat: 5.8g

Cheesy Chicken Tenders

Preparation time: 10 minutes

Cooking time: 30 minutes

Servings: 4

INGREDIENTS:

- 1 large white meat chicken breast, approximately 5-6 ounces, sliced into strips
- 1 cup of breadcrumbs (Panko brand works well)
- 2 medium-sized eggs
- Pinch of salt and pepper
- 1 tablespoon of grated or powdered parmesan cheese

DIRECTIONS:

1. Cover the basket of the oven with a lining of tin foil, leaving the edges uncovered to allow to circulate through the basket. Preheat the oven to 350 degrees. In a mixing bowl, beat the eggs until fluffy and until the yolks and whites are fully combined, and set aside. In a separate mixing bowl, combine the breadcrumbs, parmesan, salt, and pepper, and set aside. One by one, dip each piece of raw chicken into the bowl with dry ingredients, coating all sides; then submerge into the bowl with wet ingredients, then dip again into the dry ingredients. Lay the coated chicken pieces on the foil covering the oven basket, in a single flat layer.

2. Set the oven timer for 15 minutes. After 15 minutes, the oven will turn off and the chicken should be mid-way cooked and the breaded coating starting to brown. Using tongs, turn each piece of chicken over to ensure a full all over fry. Reset the oven to 320 degrees for another 15 minutes. After 15 minutes, when the oven shuts off, remove the fried chicken strips using

tongs and set them on a serving plate. Eat as soon as cool enough to handle, and enjoy!

NUTRITION:

- Calories: 278
- Fat: 15g
- Protein: 29g
- Sugar: 7g

Meat

Leg of Lamb

Preparation time: 5 minutes

Cooking time: 15 minutes

Servings: 4

INGREDIENTS:

- 1-pound lamb sirloin steaks, boneless
- 1/2 of a medium white onion, peeled
- 4 slices of ginger
- 5 cloves of garlic, peeled
- 1 teaspoon salt
- 1 teaspoon ground fennel
- 1 teaspoon garam masala
- 1 teaspoon ground cinnamon
- 1 teaspoon cayenne pepper
- 1/2 teaspoon ground cardamom

DIRECTIONS:

1. Place all the ingredients in a blender except for steaks, and then pulse until well blended.
2. Make cuts in lamb chops, place them in a large bowl, add the blended mixture, toss until coated, and then let it marinate for 30 minutes.
3. Then turn on the oven, set the temperature to 330 degrees F, and then select the oven cooking method.
4. Arrange the lamb steaks in a single layer in the oven basket and then cook for 15 minutes until cooked, flipping halfway.
5. Serve straight away.

NUTRITION:

-   Calories: 182
-   Fat: 7g
-   Carbs: 3g
-   Protein: 24g
-   Fiber: 1g

Herbed Rack of Lamb

Preparation time: 5 minutes

Cooking time: 12 minutes

Servings: 4

INGREDIENTS:

- 1 rack of lamb

For the marinade

- 2 teaspoons minced garlic
- 1 teaspoon salt
- 2 tablespoons dried rosemary
- 1 teaspoon ground black pepper
- 1 tablespoon dried thyme
- 4 tablespoons olive oil

DIRECTIONS:

1. Turn on the oven, set the temperature to 360 degrees F, and then select the oven cooking method.
2. Meanwhile, take a small bowl, place all the ingredients for the marinade, and then stir until combined.
3. Rub the marinade on all sides of the rack of lamb, place it in the oven basket, and then 10 to 12 minutes until done.
4. When done, slice the rack of lamb into pieces and then serve.

NUTRITION:

- Calories: 293
- Fat: 15g
- Carbs: 4g
- Protein: 32g
- Fiber: 1g

Rosemary and Garlic Lamb Shoulder

Preparation time: 10 minutes

Cooking time: 1 hour and 30 minutes

Servings: 8

INGREDIENTS:

- 3 pounds half lamb leg roast
- 2 cloves of garlic, slices
- 1 1/2 teaspoon salt
- 1 teaspoon ground black pepper
- 1 tablespoon dried rosemary
- 2 tablespoons olive oil

DIRECTIONS:

1. Turn on the oven, set the temperature to 400 degrees F, and then select the oven cooking method.

2. Meanwhile, make cuts in the fat side of the lamb leg and then stuff garlic into the cuts.
3. Stir together rosemary and oil, brush this mixture on the lamb and then season with salt and black pepper.
4. Arrange the lamb on the oven basket, cook it for 15 minutes, switch the temperature to 320 degrees F and continue cooking for 1 hour and 15 minutes until roasted.
5. Serve straight away.

NUTRITION:

- Calories: 205
- Fat: 9g
- Carbs: 1g
- Protein: 28g
- Fiber: 0.5g

Bread

Marvelous Chocolate Zucchini Bread

Preparation time: 20 minutes

Cooking time: 40 minutes

Servings: 2

INGREDIENTS:

- 3 medium eggs
- 1 cup sugar
- 1 cup vegetable oil
- 2 cup grated zucchini
- 1 teaspoon vanilla extract
- 3/4 cup semisweet chocolate chips
- 1/3 cup cocoa powder
- 2 cup wheat flour
- 1 teaspoon baking soda

- A pinch of salt
- 1 teaspoon ground cinnamon

DIRECTIONS:

1. Spray two baking pans with cooking spray.
2. In a medium mixing bowl, add cocoa powder, eggs, oil, grated zucchini, vanilla, and sugar. Stir to combine. Fold in flour, baking soda, salt, and cinnamon. Then, add chocolate chips.
3. Pour batter into baking pans. Bake on 1-inch rack on power level High (350°C) for 40-45 minutes until a knife inserted in the center comes out clean. Allow bread to rest inside the dome for 1-2 minutes before removing it from NuWave Oven. Allow cooling before slicing.

NUTRITION:

- Calories: 217.0
- Total Fat: 8.0g
- Total carbs: 37.0g
- Protein: 3.0g

Zucchini & Coconut Bread

Preparation time: 15 minutes

Cooking time: 3 hours

Servings: 10

INGREDIENTS:

- 2 1/2 cups zucchini, shredded
- 1/2 teaspoon salt
- 1 1/3 cups almond flour
- 2/3 cup coconut, shredded
- 2 teaspoons ground cinnamon
- 1/2 teaspoon ground ginger
- 1/4 teaspoon ground nutmeg
- 3 large organic eggs
- 1/4 cup butter, melted
- 1/4 cup water
- 1/2 teaspoon organic vanilla extract
- 1/2 cup walnuts, chopped
- 1/3 cup coconut oil
- 1 cup Erythritol
- 1/2 cup protein powder
- 1 teaspoon baking powder

DIRECTIONS:

1. Arrange a large sieve in a sink.
2. Place the zucchini in a sieve and sprinkle with salt. Set aside to drain for about 1 hour.
3. With your hands, squeeze out the moisture from zucchini.
4. In a large bowl, add the almond flour, coconut, Erythritol, protein powder, baking powder, and spices and mix well.

5. Add the zucchini, eggs, coconut oil, water, and vanilla extract and mix until well combined.
6. Fold in the walnuts.
7. At the bottom of a greased oven, place the mixture.
8. Close the oven with a crisping lid and select "Slow Cooker."
9. Set on "Low" for 21/2-3 hours.
10. Press "Start/Stop" to begin cooking.
11. Keep the bread inside for about 5-10 minutes.
12. Carefully, remove the bread from the pot and place onto a wire rack to cool completely before slicing.
13. Cut the bread into desired-sized slices and serve.

NUTRITION:

- Calories: 145
- Carbs: 3.6
- Protein: 2.1g
- Fat: 13.6g

Carrot Bread

Preparation time: 15 minutes

Cooking time: 3 hours

Servings: 12

INGREDIENTS:

- 1 cup almond flour
- 1/3 cup coconut flour
- 1 1/2 teaspoons organic baking powder
- 1 teaspoon ground cinnamon
- 1/4 teaspoon ground cloves
- 1/4 teaspoon ground nutmeg
- 1/4 teaspoon salt
- 1 cup Erythritol
- 1/3 cup coconut oil, softened
- 3 organic eggs
- 1 teaspoon organic vanilla extract
- 1/2 teaspoon organic almond extract
- 2 cups plus 2 tablespoons carrots, peeled and shredded
- 1 teaspoon baking soda

DIRECTIONS:

1. In a bowl, add the flours, baking powder, baking soda, spices, and salt and mix well.
2. In another large bowl, add the Erythritol, coconut oil, eggs, and both extracts and beat until well combined.
3. Add the flour mixture and mix until just combined.
4. Fold in the carrots.
5. Place the mixture into a greased 8x4-inch silicone bread pan.
6. Arrange a "Reversible Rack" in the pot of the oven.
7. Place the pan over the "Reversible Rack."

8. Close the oven with a crisping lid and select "Slow Cooker."
9. Set on "Low" for 3 hours.
10. Press "Start/Stop" to begin cooking.
11. Place the bread pan onto a wire rack for about 5-10 minutes.
12. Carefully, remove the bread from the pan and place it onto the wire rack to cool completely before slicing.
13. Cut the bread into desired-sized slices and serve.

NUTRITION:

- Calories: 145
- Carbs: 3.6
- Protein: 2.1g
- Fat: 13.6g

French toast

Preparation time: 15 minutes

Cooking time: 10 minutes

Servings: 4

INGREDIENTS:

- 6 eggs
- 1 cup milk
- 1 cup heavy cream
- 1 teaspoon honey
- Cooking spray
- 1 loaf French bread, sliced
- 1/2 cup butter
- 1/2 cup sugar

DIRECTIONS:

1. Beat the eggs in a bowl.
2. Stir in milk, cream, and honey.
3. Dip the bread slices into the mixture.
4. Add to the grill basket inside the oven grill.
5. Spread some butter and sprinkle sugar on top of the bread slices.
6. Seal the pot and oven at 350 degrees F for 5 to 10 minutes.
7. Serve with maple syrup.

Tip: It's a good idea to use day-old bread for this recipe.

NUTRITION:

- Calories: 145
- Carbs: 3.6,
- Protein: 2.1g
- Fat: 13.6g

Cake & Dessert

Plum Cake

Preparation time: 10 minutes

Cooking time: 30 minutes

Servings: 8

INGREDIENTS:

- 1/2 cup butter, soft
- 3 eggs
- 1/2 cup swerve
- 1/4 teaspoon almond extract
- 1 tablespoon vanilla extract
- 1 and 1/2 cups almond flour
- 1/2 cup coconut flour
- 2 teaspoons baking powder
- 3/4 cup almond milk

- 4 plums, pitted and chopped

DIRECTIONS:

1. In a bowl, mix all the ingredients and whisk well.
2. Pour this into a cake pan that fits the oven after you've lined it with parchment paper, put the pan in the machine and cook at 370 degrees F for 30 minutes.
3. Cool the cake down, slice and serve.

NUTRITION:

- Calories: 183
- Fat: 4g
- Fiber: 3g
- Carbs: 4g
- Protein: 7g

Christmas Magic Bars

Preparation time: 10 minutes

Cooking time: 25 minutes

Servings: 4

INGREDIENTS:

- 1/3 cup melted salted butter
- 1 1/2 cups of chocolate baking crumbs
- 1 300ml can of dulce de leche condensed milk (sweetened)
- 1 1/2 cups flaked unsweetened coconut
- 1 cup of red and green Christmas cherries chopped
- 1 cup of semi-sweet chocolate chips

DIRECTIONS:

1. Preheat your oven to 350 degrees F.
2. Pour the butter into an 8x8 pan. If wanted, line the pan with tinfoil first for easier removal.
3. Sprinkle the baking crumbs on top of the butter in an even layer.
4. Drop the condensed milk onto the crumbs by the spoonful, creating an even layer of it.
5. Sprinkle the 3 remaining ingredients, in the order given over the condensed milk. Press down gently.
6. Bake in the oven for 25-30 minutes until the coconut has browned.
7. Remove and cool completely in the pan before slicing. To remove, use the tinfoil to take it out, then slice.

NUTRITION:

- Calories: 193
- Fat: 5g
- Fiber: 1g
- Carbs: 4g
- Protein: 4g

Vanilla Pound Cake

Preparation time: 35 minutes

Cooking time: 15 minutes

Servings: 6

INGREDIENTS:

- 1/2 cup full-fat sour cream
- 1 oz. full-fat cream cheese; softened
- 2 large eggs
- 1/2 cup granular erythritol
- 1 cup blanched finely ground almond flour
- 1/4 cup salted butter; melted
- 1 teaspoon baking powder
- 1 teaspoon vanilla extract

DIRECTIONS:

1. Take a large bowl, mix almond flour, butter and erythritol.
2. Add in vanilla, baking powder, sour cream and cream cheese and mix until well combined. Add eggs and mix.
3. Pour batter into a 6-inch round baking pan. Place pan into the oven basket. Adjust the temperature to 300 Degrees F and set the timer for 25 minutes.
4. When the cake is done, a toothpick inserted in center will come out clean. The center should not feel wet. Allow it to cool completely, or the cake will crumble when moved.

NUTRITION:

- Calories: 253g
- Protein: 6.9g
- Fiber: 2.0g
- Fat: 22.6g
- Carbs: 25.2g

Mini Lava Cakes

Preparation time: 30 minutes

Cooking time: 15 minutes

Servings: 4

INGREDIENTS:

- 3 oz. dark chocolate; melted
- 2 eggs, whisked
- 1/4 cup coconut oil; melted
- 1 tablespoon almond flour
- 2 tablespoon swerve
- 1/4 teaspoon vanilla extract
- Cooking spray

DIRECTIONS:

1. In a bowl, combine all the ingredients except the cooking spray and whisk really well.
2. Divide this into 4 ramekins greased with cooking spray, put them in the oven, and cook at 360°F for 20 minutes

NUTRITION:

- Calories: 161
- Fat: 12g
- Fiber: 1g
- Carbs: 4g
- Protein: 7g

Lemon Blackberries Cake

Preparation time: 35 minutes

Cooking time: 15 minutes

Servings: 4

INGREDIENTS:

- 2 eggs, whisked
- 1/4 cup almond milk
- 1 1/2 cups almond flour
- 1 cup blackberries; chopped
- 2 tablespoon ghee; melted
- 4 tablespoon swerve
- 1 teaspoon lemon zest, grated
- 1 teaspoon lemon juice
- 1/2 teaspoon baking powder

DIRECTIONS:

1. Take a bowl and mix all the ingredients and whisk well.
2. Pour this into a cake pan that fits the oven lined with parchment paper, put the pan in your oven, and cook at 340°F for 25 minutes. Cool the cake down, slice, and serve

NUTRITION:

- Calories: 193
- Fat: 5g
- Fiber: 1g
- Carbs: 4g
- Protein: 4g

Yogurt Cake

Preparation time: 35 minutes

Cooking time: 15 minutes

Servings: 12

INGREDIENTS:

- 6 eggs, whisked
- 8 oz. Greek yogurt
- 9 oz. coconut flour
- 4 tablespoon stevia
- 1 teaspoon vanilla extract
- 1 teaspoon baking powder

DIRECTIONS:

1. Take a bowl and mix all the ingredients and whisk well.

2. Pour this into a cake pan that fits the oven lined with parchment paper.
3. Put the pan in the oven and cook at 330°F for 30 minutes

NUTRITION:

- Calories: 181
- Fat: 13g
- Fiber: 2g
- Carbs: 4g
- Protein: 5g

Chocolate Coffee Cake

Preparation time: 40 minutes

Cooking time: 15 minutes

Servings: 8

INGREDIENTS:

- 1 1/2 cups almond flour
- 1/2 cup coconut meal
- 2/3 cup swerve
- 1 teaspoon baking powder
- 1/4 teaspoon salt
- 1 stick butter, melted
- 1/2 cup hot strongly brewed coffee
- 1/2 teaspoon vanilla
- 1 egg

Topping

- 1/4 cup coconut flour
- 1/2 cup confectioner's swerve
- 1/2 teaspoon ground cardamom
- 1 teaspoon ground cinnamon
- 3 tablespoons coconut oil

DIRECTIONS:

1. Mix all dry ingredients for your cake; then, mix in the wet ingredients. Mix until everything is well incorporated.
2. Spritz a baking pan with cooking spray. Scrape the batter into the baking pan.
3. Then, make the topping by mixing all ingredients. Place on top of the cake. Smooth the top with a spatula.

4. Bake at 330 degrees F for 30 minutes or until the top of the cake springs back when gently pressed with your fingers. Serve with your favorite hot beverage.

NUTRITION:

- Calories: 285
- Fat: 21g
- Carbs: 6g
- Protein: 8g
- Sugars: 3g
- Fiber: 1g

Measurement Conversion Chart

American and British Variances					
Term	**Abbreviation**	**Nationality**	**Dry or liquid**	**Metric equivalent**	**Equivalent in context**
cup	c., C.		usually liquid	237 milliliters	16 tablespoons or 8 ounces
ounce	fl oz, fl. oz.	American	liquid only	29.57 milliliters	
		British	either	28.41 milliliters	
gallon	gal.	American	liquid only	3.785 liters	4 quarts
		British	either	4.546 liters	4 quarts
inch	in, in.			2.54 centimeters	
ounce	oz, oz.	American	dry	28.35 grams	1/16 pound
			liquid	see OUNCE	see OUNCE
pint	p., pt.	American	liquid	0.473 liter	1/8 gallon or 16 ounces
			dry	0.551 liter	1/2 quart
		British	either	0.568 liter	
pound	lb.		dry	453.592 grams	16 ounces
Quart	q., qt, qt.	American	liquid	0.946 liter	1/4 gallon or 32 ounces
			dry	1.101 liters	2 pints
		British	either	1.136 liters	
Teaspoon	t., tsp., tsp		either	about 5 milliliters	1/3 tablespoon
Tablespoon	T., tbs., tbsp.		either	about 15 milliliters	3 teaspoons or 1/2 ounce

Volume (Liquid)

American Standard (Cups & Quarts)	American Standard (Ounces)	Metric (Milliliters & Liters)
2 tbsp.	1 fl. oz.	30 ml
1/4 cup	2 fl. oz.	60 ml
1/2 cup	4 fl. oz.	125 ml
1 cup	8 fl. oz.	250 ml
1 1/2 cups	12 fl. oz.	375 ml
2 cups or 1 pint	16 fl. oz.	500 ml
4 cups or 1 quart	32 fl. oz.	1000 ml or 1 liter
1 gallon	128 fl. oz.	4 liters

Volume (Dry)

American Standard	Metric
1/8 teaspoon	5 ml
1/4 teaspoon	1 ml
1/2 teaspoon	2 ml
3/4 teaspoon	4 ml
1 teaspoon	5 ml
1 tablespoon	15 ml
1/4 cup	59 ml
1/3 cup	79 ml
1/2 cup	118 ml
2/3 cup	158 ml
3/4 cup	177 ml
1 cup	225 ml
2 cups or 1 pint	450 ml
3 cups	675 ml
4 cups or 1 quart	1 liter
1/2 gallon	2 liters
1 gallon	4 liters

Dry Measure Equivalents

3 teaspoons	1 tablespoon	1/2 ounce	14.3 grams
2 tablespoons	1/8 cup	1 ounce	28.3 grams
4 tablespoons	1/4 cup	2 ounces	56.7 grams
5 1/3 tablespoons	1/3 cup	2.6 ounces	75.6 grams
8 tablespoons	1/2 cup	4 ounces	113.4 grams
12 tablespoons	3/4 cup	6 ounces	.375 pound
32 tablespoons	2 cups	16 ounces	1 pound

Oven Temperatures

American Standard	Metric
250° F	130° C
300° F	150° C
350° F	180° C
400° F	200° C
450° F	230° C

Weight (Mass)

American Standard (Ounces)	Metric (Grams)
1/2 ounce	15 grams
1 ounce	30 grams
3 ounces	85 grams
3.75 ounces	100 grams
4 ounces	115 grams
8 ounces	225 grams
12 ounces	340 grams
16 ounces or 1 pound	450 grams

Lightning Source UK Ltd.
Milton Keynes UK
UKHW020813150321
380363UK00001B/21